Polar Bears

By Dr. Hugh Roome

Children's Press®
An Imprint of Scholastic Inc.

Content Consultants
Carrie Pratt
Curator, North America and Polar Frontier
Columbus Zoo and Aquarium

Devon Sabo
Zoo Keeper, North America and Polar Frontier
Columbus Zoo and Aquarium

Library of Congress Cataloging-in-Publication Data

Names: Roome, Hugh, author.
Title: Polar bears/by Dr. Hugh Roome.
Description: New York, NY: Children's Press, an Imprint of Scholastic Inc., 2018. |
Series: Nature's children | Includes index.
Identifiers: LCCN 2017041062| ISBN 9780531234846 (library binding) | ISBN 9780531245149 (pbk.)
Subjects: LCSH: Polar bear—Juvenile literature.
Classification: LCC QL737.C27 R66 2018 | DDC 599.786—dc23
LC record available at https://lccn.loc.gov/2017041062

Design by Anna Tunick Tabachnik

Creative Direction: Judith Christ-Lafond for Scholastic

Produced by Spooky Cheetah Press

Printed in China 62

SCHOLASTIC, CHILDREN'S PRESS, NATURE'S CHILDREN™, and associated logos
are trademarks and/or registered trademarks of Scholastic Inc.

2 3 4 5 6 7 8 9 10 R 27 26 25 24 23 22 21 20 19 18

Scholastic Inc., 557 Broadway, New York, NY 10012.

Photographs ©: cover main: Sylvain Cordier/Minden Pictures; cover background: hauged/iStockphoto;
1: J Marshall-Tribaleye Images/Alamy Images; 4 leaf silo and throughout: stockgraphicdesigns.com; 5 bottom: Wayne R.
Bilenduke/Getty Images; 5 child silo: All-Silhouettes.com; 5 polar bear silo and throughout: LANTERIA/Shutterstock;
7: MyLoupe/UIG via Getty Images; 8-9: Steven Kazlowski/Minden Pictures; 10: Flip Nicklin/Minden Pictures; 11: Wayne Lynch/
Getty Images; 12-13: Stuart & Michele Westmorland/Getty Images; 15 main: SeppFriedhuber/iStockphoto; 15 inset: Tui De Roy/
Minden Pictures; 16-17: Rob Reijnen/Minden Pictures; 18-19: Paul Souders/AWLimages; 21: Michael Nolan/robertharding/Getty
Images; 22-23: Per-Gunnar Ostby/Getty Images; 24-25: Wayne Lynch/Getty Images; 26-27: Matthias Breiter/Minden Pictures;
28-29: Sylvain Cordier/Getty Images; 31: Hemis/Alamy Images; 32-33: zixian/Shutterstock; 35: Andreas Weith/Wikimedia;
36: Paul Nicklen/National Geographic Creative; 38-39: Robert Harding Picture Library/Superstock; 40-41: Jan Martin Will/
Shutterstock; 42 bottom: Martin Mecnarowski/Shutterstock; 42 top left: Eric Isselee/Shutterstock; 42 top center: Sonsedska
Yuliia/Shutterstock; 42 top right: Sombra12/Dreamstime; 43 bottom: Katherine Feng/Minden Pictures; 43 top left: taden/
iStockphoto; 43 top center: Andyworks/iStockphoto; 43 top right: Wayne Lynch/Getty Images.

Maps by Jim McMahon.

Table of Contents

Fact File: Polar Bears

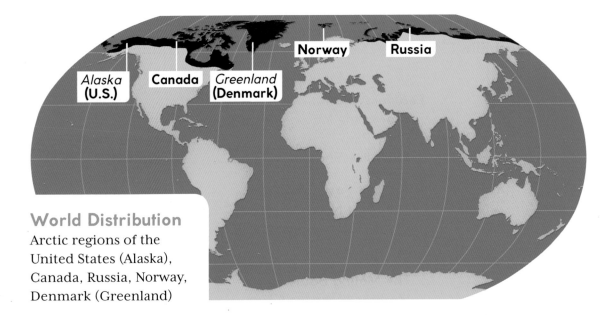

Norway
Russia

Alaska (U.S.)
Canada
Greenland (Denmark)

World Distribution
Arctic regions of the
United States (Alaska),
Canada, Russia, Norway,
Denmark (Greenland)

Population Status
Vulnerable

Habitat
Freezing Arctic
region, including
the North Pole

Habits
Hunt almost
constantly; can
swim for days in
icy water; mostly
solitary; mothers
usually have two
cubs and give birth
in snow caves

Diet
Mainly seals; also
walruses, caribou,
fish, ducks, foxes,
and kelp

Distinctive Features
Whitish fur;
huge feet for
walking on snow
and swimming;
massive body with
pointy-shaped
nose and head

Fast Fact
Male polar bears
are two times as
big as females.

Average Size

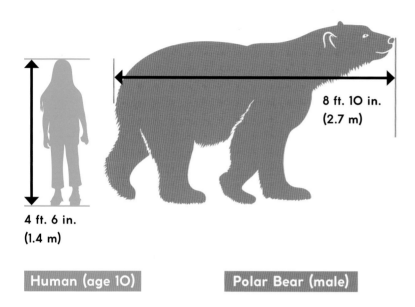

4 ft. 6 in.
(1.4 m)

8 ft. 10 in.
(2.7 m)

Human (age 10)   Polar Bear (male)

◀ For the first years
of their lives, cubs are
completely dependent
on their mother.

CHAPTER 1

Fearless Giant

At the frigid North Pole, temperatures can drop to -70°F (-56.7°C) and the wind can blow with hurricane force for days. But that is not a problem for the King of the **Arctic**. The polar bear is perfectly **adapted** to this frozen world. In fact, another name for this massive **carnivore** is ice bear.

A polar bear is the strongest, fiercest animal on Earth! How can it be, then, that this magnificent animal is in danger of becoming **extinct**?

Polar bears depend on the **sea ice** for their survival. That's where, when the ice is at its thickest, the polar bear hunts its favorite **prey**: seals.

Because of **climate change**, the ice is forming later and melting earlier every year. That gives polar bears less time to hunt. Many bears must return to land without having had enough to eat.

▶ A male polar bear can stand up to 10 feet (3.1 meters) tall.

Life on the Ice

The polar bear's Arctic **habitat** is hundreds of square miles of desolate, frozen wilderness. Sometimes the bears have to swim for miles in freezing water to reach new hunting grounds. But that's no problem for the polar bear, whose scientific name, *Ursus maritimus*, means sea bear.

Polar bears are huge. Large males weigh about 1,500 pounds (680.4 kilograms). And they are protected by the most incredible coat. It keeps the bears warm—and provides **camouflage** for hunting. Although the polar bear's fur looks white, it is actually **transparent**. The way the fur reflects sunlight makes it look white—just like the bear's snowy surroundings. A polar bear's fur is oily and slicks down against its body for smooth swimming.

Underneath the polar bear's heavy fur coat is a layer of fat that is 4 inches (10.2 centimeters) thick. The Arctic cold cannot get through this barrier. And when the bear swims, the fat helps it float. On the flip side, polar bears don't have much tolerance for warm weather.

◀ Polar bears usually walk at a leisurely pace so they don't overheat.

Body Plan

Polar bears live under the harshest conditions on Earth—and that's not only because of the weather. Finding food is a constant struggle. And when two males come into conflict—whether they're fighting over prey or a mate—the results can be deadly. Luckily, this bear is built for survival.

Polar bears can stand tall when confronting other bears. Their claws, which are ideal for digging in snow and ice, are also deadly weapons. These bears can strike with lightning speed to wound an enemy or kill prey. They also have 42 razor-sharp teeth, which are designed to tear into their victims.

Front Paws

have tiny depressions that act like suction cups when the bear walks on ice.

Fast Fact
Polar bears have 10 more teeth than humans do.

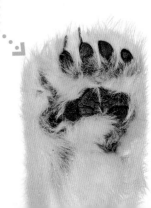

Nose gives polar bears a very keen sense of smell. It is one of the few areas of skin that is not covered in fur.

Ears are small and round to help minimize heat loss.

Black Skin (found underneath fur) soaks up the heat of the sun.

Fur provides camouflage in the polar bear's Arctic habitat.

Claws are more than 5 in. (12.7 cm) long.

Paws like Snowshoes

A polar bear's paws are not like other bears' paws. They are much, much bigger—about 12 in. (30.5 cm) across. That's about the size of a dinner plate!

The paws act like snowshoes, helping the polar bear walk on top of soft snow instead of sinking into it. Likewise, the big paws spread out the polar bear's weight to keep the animal from breaking through thin sea ice.

The bottom sides of the paws, called the pads, are covered in bumps and lined with fur. Both features keep the polar bears from slipping and skidding on the ice.

Polar bears' slightly webbed paws also help them swim. The paws work like paddles in the water.

▶ When a polar bear swims, it uses its back feet for steering.

CHAPTER 2

Huge but Fast

If you saw a polar bear walking along the ice, you would notice that it shuffles along slowly. If you saw it swim, you would think it was doing a lazy dog paddle. But don't be fooled. Polar bears can run and swim a lot faster than you! They can race along at 25 miles per hour (40.2 kilometers per hour)—the same speed as a car driving through town. And they can swim at 6 mph (9.7 kph)—and keep up that pace all day without stopping.

However, polar bears do not swim or run fast enough to catch their dinner. Most land animals in the Arctic, such as foxes and caribou, can outrun them. Most of the seals, walruses, and narwhals that the bears want to eat can swim faster, too. So this clever **predator** has had to come up with other techniques for hunting.

▶ A polar bear's claws don't retract, or pull back into its paws. That helps the bear walk on slippery ice.

▲ The ringed seal is one of the polar bear's favorite meals.

The Hunt Never Stops

There is not much to eat in the polar bears' habitat. The bears look for food everywhere they go. To keep healthy, polar bears hunt constantly during the winter months. They need to eat great amounts of meat each day. The best place to hunt seals is on sea ice, which the bears use as a hunting platform.

Seals are **mammals** that mainly live in the ocean. They swim under the ice but must come up periodically to breathe. To do so, the seals make holes in the ice from under the water throughout their range.

Because polar bears can't use speed to catch their prey, they rely on **stealth**. First the bear uses smell to find where the seal lives. A polar bear can smell a seal's breathing hole in the ice from more than 1 mile (1.6 kilometers) away! The bear slowly creeps up to where the seal will come up for air. Then it lies flat on the ice and waits—keeping perfectly still for hours and hours if necessary—until the seal comes up for air. When it does, the polar bear attacks, snatching the seal from the water and dragging it onto the ice.

◀ Ringed seals have the fat and calories polar bears need to stay healthy.

Long-Distance Swimmer

Sometimes a polar bear has to swim to find better places to hunt. But it cannot hunt very well while swimming. Seals are much faster swimmers and can dive much deeper than a polar bear can. Instead, the bear will search for an **ice floe** to use as a hunting platform.

The polar bear can swim all day between blocks of ice. In fact, scientists followed one bear in Alaska's Bering Strait that swam 400 mi. (643.7 km) in nine days. This is when the bear's build makes a difference. Its fur gets slick in water—like a wet suit. And its fat is **buoyant**, like a life vest, so the bear doesn't have to make an effort to keep its head above water.

Most of a bear's hunts are unsuccessful. The seals usually get away. But the polar bear will hunt on the sea ice nonstop for months at a time and eat many, many seals.

▶ As sea ice shrinks, polar bears are forced to swim farther to find prey.

CHAPTER 3

A Bear's Life

Male polar bears are ready to mate when they reach maturity—anywhere from six to 10 years old. Females are ready a little earlier—when they are around four to six years old.

Most of the time, polar bears are **solitary**. Male and female polar bears hunt alone across large areas of their Arctic habitat. When a female bear is old enough to have babies, male bears will track her down—literally following the female for as far as 60 mi. (96.6 km).

When the male and female meet, they play together. But scientists believe that the playing is actually a test. The female bear leads the male up and down mountains and across the ice to make sure that he is strong and healthy. When the female is satisfied that the male is fit enough to father her cubs, the two stay together for one or two weeks to mate.

▶ A male polar bear follows the scent trail left by a female bear's footpads.

The Mating Battle

During the two weeks spent mating, the male bear is in for big trouble. Other male bears will come along to try to mate with the female. The bear that has partnered with the female must defend himself from several different bears who will attack him.

Battles between male bears are violent and fierce. When two males fight each other, they stand tall on their hind legs and growl ferociously before attacking. They use their paws to try to knock each other down and claw each other bloody. They bite each other's face and legs if they can. At the end of the mating period, the bears are scarred and bloody and often have broken teeth and other injuries. The males then leave the female and each other to set out alone again on the Arctic ice.

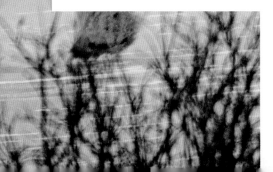

◀ If a polar bear damages its teeth in a fight, it will have a hard time surviving.

Mothers Make Ice Caves

After the male bear leaves the female, she prepares for her pregnancy by eating as much as she can. Then, in late fall to early winter, she makes a **den**. She uses her massive paws and sharp claws to create an ice cave for her babies. First she digs a burrow, or hole, in a snowbank. Then she packs the snow into a room. The female settles into the cave and waits for fresh snowfall to close off the entrance. The thick snow and ice of the cave protect her from the wind and the worst of the Arctic cold. The ice cave provides her with a safe place to have her babies.

Unlike most other kinds of bears, polar bears do not **hibernate**. However, as she waits to give birth, the female goes into a deep resting phase. She starts breathing slowly and barely moves because she needs to conserve energy. Her heartbeat slows from 42 to only 27 beats per minute.

Most polar bear babies, called cubs, are born in December. The mother may give birth to one, two, or three cubs, but twins are most common.

▶ Inside this den, the temperature may be 40°F (4.4°C) warmer than it is outside.

Tiny, Helpless Cubs

Polar bear cubs weigh only 1 lb. (0.45 kg) at birth. They are born blind and with barely any fur. The cubs grow strong on their mother's milk. They will continue to **nurse** for up to two years.

By the time the bears leave the den when the cubs are two to three months old, the mother is almost starving. She has not eaten at all the entire time she's been in the den. She needs to get food for herself, and the cubs are ready to start eating solid food, too.

The mother bear breaks out a wall of the cave and pulls herself into the daylight. The cubs scramble out behind her. They have only lived in a dark, tiny space. For them everything is new! Sun! Walking! Snow! They immediately follow their mother. She is headed to the sea ice to hunt seals. She must find food now.

◀ Cubs learn survival skills by copying their mother.

From Cub to King of the Arctic

The mother polar bear has so much to do to help her cubs survive. Half of all cubs die before they are one year old. The cubs' mother will do anything within her power to help them stay alive.

For the first two weeks after breaking open the cave, the mother and her cubs stay near the den. The cubs follow their mother as she hunts. They are learning to walk on the ice. The cubs make a game of pretending they are hunting, too. They play fight, having fun while learning to defend themselves. This form of play helps the cubs get ready for a life spent mostly alone.

The mother bear shelters her cubs from the wind. When she needs to swim between hunting areas, she carries them on her back. If anyone threatens her cubs, the mother bear puts them behind her and defends them with her life!

After about two years, the cubs are big and strong enough to be on their own. The mother bear abandons them or even chases them away. The youngsters are ready to assume their role as the most powerful animal on Earth.

▶ Even mature bears sometimes play fight.

CHAPTER 4

An Ancient Family

Polar bears are part of a family of mammals that **evolved** millions of years ago—yes, the bear family. How are polar bears like other bears?

All bears have heavy fur coats, huge bones, powerful legs, stub tails, and paws with claws for hunting and digging. They all walk the same way—with a kind of shuffle. They all can stand up on two legs to fight. And all bears except pandas can run fast when they need to.

Polar bear **ancestors** go back over 35 million years. **Fossils** show that these ancient brown bears were big—but not much bigger than a male polar bear.

Scientists believe that polar bears became different from their brown bear ancestors about 600,000 years ago. Analysis of bear fossils shows that the bears of the Arctic survived because of special adaptations that set them apart from their brown bear cousins.

▶ This is the skeleton of a cave bear, a species that went extinct 20,000 years ago.

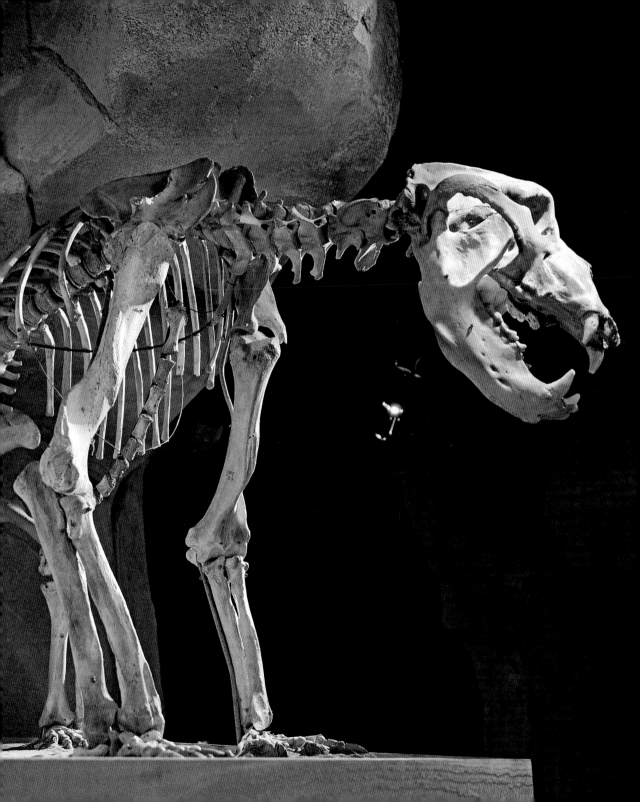

Close Cousins

The **DNA** of a brown bear is very close to that of a polar bear. There are many types of brown bear.

Grizzly bears live inland among forests and mountains. The dark color of their fur is camouflage in the woods. They eat everything from insects to roots and grasses. They chase down young caribou, rabbits, and squirrels.

Another type is the Kodiak bear, which lives on islands off the coast of Alaska. Kodiak bears are huge. They can reach heights of 10 ft. (3.1 m) tall. But most brown bears are only half the size of the polar bear.

Like polar bears, brown bears are powerful. An adult brown bear has been known to kill a bison with one blow from its paw. But brown bears can't survive in the Arctic!

Both male and female brown bears build dens to wait out winter. They dig a burrow and make a sort of cave. Then they hibernate to conserve energy. That's another difference between brown bears and polar bears.

◀ Salmon is a favorite food of brown bears that live in Alaska.

CHAPTER 5

The Warming Arctic

Fewer than 30,000 ice bears are left

in the world. That's because climate change is destroying the sea ice where they find most of their food.

Sea ice grows and shrinks with the seasons. It is at its smallest during the month of September. Scientists at the National Aeronautics and Space Administration (NASA) have discovered that September sea ice is shrinking by 13 percent every decade.

If there is no sea ice, polar bears have nowhere to hunt. If they can't catch seals, they will have to find other food to eat. And that's not easy.

The question for survival is whether polar bears can adapt to a new diet. Some scientists believe two-thirds of all polar bears will die off in the next 30 years because of the loss of sea ice and lack of access to prey!

▶ Polar bears that can't access prey face death by starvation.

Working to Save Polar Bears

The scientists who study polar bears have learned that when they can't find enough seals, the bears try to eat more whales and walruses. They go after more fish and ducks. They'll try eating almost anything, including geese, caribou, berries, and kelp. Hungry polar bears even go to garbage dumps in nearby towns where they eat all kinds of human trash, including motor oil.

Scientists from the U.S. Geological Survey Changing Arctic Ecosystems initiative are studying polar bears to measure the impact of warmer temperatures. They **sedate** bears and then check their health, particularly to see what they are eating. The scientists put **transmitters** on some bears so they can track them by satellite. They try to count all the polar bears to see if their numbers are in decline. Sadly, the scientists are spotting more starving polar bears. Polar bears usually live to about 18 years old in the wild. Now, in Alaska, fewer cubs grow up to be adults.

◀ Researchers check on a bear that has been sedated.

Polar Bear Hunters

For thousands of years, polar bears have been hunted by native people living in the Arctic—not for sport but for sustenance. These hunters use almost every bit of the bear. They eat the meat and fat and make pants and boots from the hide. The native people use spears and arrows to hunt the bears, and they do not kill many. Things changed when non-native people from countries with land in the Arctic—Russia, Norway, Denmark, Canada, and the United States—started hunting polar bears, too.

These new hunters might shoot a polar bear from an airplane or a helicopter or even an icebreaker. They chase down the bears with snowmobiles and shoot them with powerful rifles from a safe distance. The use of guns and machines resulted in many more bears being killed.

Great news: The governments of the countries where polar bears live got together and made a deal to restrict the hunting. They created laws that limit the number of polar bears that can be shot for sport, while still allowing the native people to kill some bears.

▶ Native hunters might use dogs to corner a bear before killing it.

Help Save Our Polar Bears

There are many people studying the polar bear problem. And there are many groups, such as the U.S. Geological Survey Polar Bear Team, the World Wildlife Fund, Polar Bears International, and the U.S. Fish and Wildlife Service, that are working to save these magnificent bears.

In fact, the international effort by the United States, Norway, Canada, Russia, and Denmark to control sport hunting of polar bears has made a huge difference. It shows us that good people working together from around the world can begin to save **vulnerable** animals.

The effects of climate change in the Arctic are harder to deal with. But we can all help. We all need to work to reduce the pollution we humans put into the air and water that contributes to climate change.

Learning about polar bears and supporting the efforts of our government and groups that work to help the bears survive can make a huge difference, as well.

◀ This polar bear is running out of hunting platforms.

Polar Bear Family Tree

Polar bears are mammals. Mammals are warm-blooded animals that have hair or fur and usually give birth to live babies; female mammals produce milk to feed their young. Mammals comprise more than 5,000 species. They all share a common ancestor that lived 100 million years ago. This diagram shows how polar bears are related to some other mammals and, specifically, to other types of bears. The closer together two animals are on the tree, the more similar they are.

Raccoons
small mammals with black eye markings and long striped tails

Red Pandas
raccoon-like mammals with reddish fur and long, bushy tails

Seals
heavy swimming mammals with flippers for limbs

Dogs
medium-sized mammals with strong jaws and a sharp sense of smell

Ancestor of all Mammals

Note: Animal photos are not to scale.

Brown Bears
large meat-
and plant-
eating bears

Black Bears
large, mostly
plant-eating
bears with black
fur and tall ears

Polar Bears
large meat-
eating bears
with white fur
and wide paws
for paddling
through water

Giant Pandas
bears with thick
coats, wide paws,
and flat teeth for
chewing bamboo

Words to Know

A .... **adapted** *(ad-ap-TED)* changed or improved to better fit into one's environment

ancestors *(ANN-sess-tuhrs)* family members who lived long ago

Arctic *(AHRK-tik)* the area around the North Pole

B .... **buoyant** *(BOI-uhnt)* able to float or stay afloat

C .... **camouflage** *(KAM-uh-flahzh)* a disguise or a natural coloring that allows animals, people, or objects to hide by making them look like their surroundings

carnivore *(KAHR-nuh-vor)* animal that eats meat

climate change *(KLYE-mat chaynj)* global warming and other changes in weather and weather patterns that are happening because of human activity

D .... **den** *(DEN)* the home of a wild animal

DNA *(DEE-en-AY)* the molecule that carries our genes, found inside the nucleus of cells

E .... **evolved** *(i-VAHLVD)* changed slowly and naturally over time

extinct *(ik-STINGKT)* no longer found alive

F .... **fossils** *(FAH-suhls)* bones, shells, or other traces of an animal or plant from millions of years ago, preserved as rock

H .... **habitat** *(HAB-i-tat)* the place where an animal or plant is usually found

hibernate *(HYE-bur-nayt)* when animals hibernate, they sleep for the entire winter; this protects them and helps them survive when the temperatures are cold and food is hard to find

I .... ice floe *(ISE FLOH)* a flat free mass of floating sea ice

M .... mammals *(MAM-uhlz)* warm-blooded animals that have hair or fur and usually give birth to live babies; female mammals produce milk to feed their young

N .... nurse *(NURS)* to drink milk from a breast

P .... predator *(PRED-uh-tuhr)* an animal that lives by hunting other animals for food

prey *(PRAY)* an animal that is hunted by another animal for food

S .... sea ice *(SEE ISE)* ice formed by the freezing of seawater; masses of floating ice that have drifted to sea

sedate *(seh-DAYT)* put to sleep using drugs

solitary *(SAH-li-ter-ee)* not requiring or without the companionship of others

stealth *(STELTH)* a way of moving characterized by silence, secrecy, and caution

sustenance *(SUHS-tuh-nuhns)* the food and drink that someone requires to live; nourishment

T .... transmitters *(trans-MIT-uhrs)* devices that send out radio or television signals

transparent *(trans-PAIR-uhnt)* clear like glass and allowing light to shine through

V .... vulnerable *(VUHL-nur-uh-buhl)* a species that is facing threats and is likely to become endangered

Find Out More

BOOKS

- Bodden, Valerie. *Polar Bears (Amazing Animals Series)*. Mankato, MN: The Creative Company, 2010.
- deSeve, Karen, and Nancy Castaldo. *National Geographic Kids Mission: Polar Bear Rescue: All About Polar Bears and How to Save Them*. Washington, D.C.: National Geographic Children's Books, 2014.
- Rosing, Norbert, and Elizabeth Carney. *Face to Face with Polar Bears*. Washington, D.C.: National Geographic Children's Books, 2007.

WEB PAGES

- www.polarbearsinternational.org
  A wealth of materials on polar bears from Polar Bears International.
- www.bearbiology.com/iba/bears-of-the-world/polar-bear
  Information on the biology of the polar bear, from the International Association for Bear Research and Management.
- www.explore.org/livecams/polar-bears/polar-bear-cape-churchill-cam-2
  Live video streams from Webcams in Canada's Wapusk National Park.

Facts for Now

Visit this Scholastic Web site for more information on polar bears:
www.factsfornow.scholastic.com Enter the keywords **Polar Bears**

Index

Index *(continued)*

About the Author

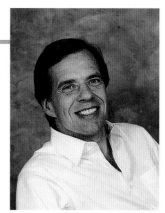

Dr. Hugh Roome is publisher of *Scholastic News*, *Science World*, and *The New York Times Upfront*. He holds a doctorate from Tufts University. This book is dedicated to the staff of the Tufts Wildlife Clinic at the Cummings School of Veterinary Medicine, where Hugh is a member of the Board of Advisors.